Heroes of the Spanish Reformation

DON CARLOS DE SESO

Heroes of the
Spanish Reformation

DON CARLOS DE SESO

STEVEN R. MARTINS

Don Carlos de Seso (c. 1515—1559), a nobleman, came from a beautiful city called Verona in Italy.

Don Carlos is known for helping so many people in the rediscovery of the *true* faith after many years of false teaching by the Roman Catholic Church.

Don Carlos was married to a very important lady named Donna Isabella. She was related to royalty in a place called Castile and Leon.

Don Carlos and Donna Isabella lived happily in a city named Valladolid in Spain.

While they lived there, Don Carlos met some friends who told him about the Reformation.

The Reformation was a movement to recover and teach the truth of God's Word, and Don Carlos thought it was a great idea!

He believed so much in these new truths, *which were always truths*, that he started sharing them with others in a town called Toro, Spain, where he served as mayor.

He even helped start a secret church where people could learn about these recovered truths.

What did the Reformation teach? That we can only be saved by God's *grace* alone, through *faith* alone, in *Christ* alone, according to the *Word* alone, for the *glory of God* alone.

But not everyone liked these recovered truths. The people of the counter-reformation, called the *Spanish Inquisition*, did not agree with Don Carlos. They took him away and asked him many questions.

Don Carlos was very brave. He wrote down what he believed and shared it with them, saying it was what he truly believed because it was plainly taught by God's Word.

Sadly, Don Carlos had to say goodbye to the world when he was only forty-three years old.

Some people thought he was wrong, but he was a hero of the true faith because he defended the truth of God's Word.

FOR PARENTS

Don Carlos de Seso (c. 1515-1559) was an Italian nobleman from Verona, and an instrumental contributor towards the advancement of the protestant, reformed faith in Spain. Being a man of high prestige, he received in marriage a Spanish lady of exceptionally high rank, Donna Isabella de Castilla, a descendent of the royal family of Castile and Leon, as a result of the favour he was shown by King Charles V of Spain for the important services he rendered to the crown. Taking up residence in Valladolid, Spain, he was exposed to the principles of the protestant reformation by engaging with the protestants of the city, and having adopted the principles himself, he became a fierce supporter of the protestant cause by promoting the reformation in Toro, where he was once *corregidor* (mayor). The result of his efforts was the founding of an underground protestant church, and was also useful in propagating reformational principles in other regions of Spain. The high status that he held, however, did not protect him from religious persecution, for as a protestant he was apprehended by the Spanish Inquisition and thrown into the secret prisons in Valladolid. After having been interrogated, which took place on the 28th of June 1558, he asked for paper, pen, and ink which led his captors to think that he was going to pen a confession, repenting of his protestant convictions. Instead, he wrote his confession of faith, and when handing it to the officer, he said "This is the true faith of the gospel, as opposed to that of the church of Rome which has been corrupted for ages: in this faith I wish to die, and in the remembrance and lively belief of the passion of Jesus Christ, to offer to God my body now reduced so low." He was burned at the stake and died at the age of fortythree, in the eyes of the public he died as a heretic, but in the eyes of God and the true church he died as a martyr.

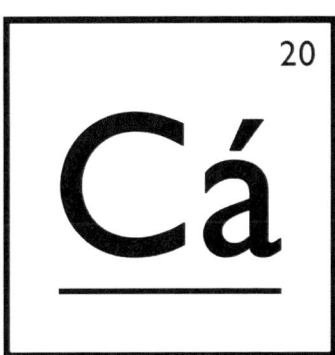

The Cántaro Institute is a reformed evangelical
organization committed to the advancement of
the Christian worldview for the reformation
and renewal of the church and culture.

www.ingramcontent.com/pod-product-compliance
Lightning Source LLC
Chambersburg PA
CBRC090830120626
46547CB00008B/643

Heroes of the Spanish Reformation is a series that surveys the lives of the brave men who risked their lives, and some who gave them up, to advance the truth of God's Word for the glory of God alone.

cántaro
publications

ISBN 978-1-990771-46-0

90000

9 781990 771460

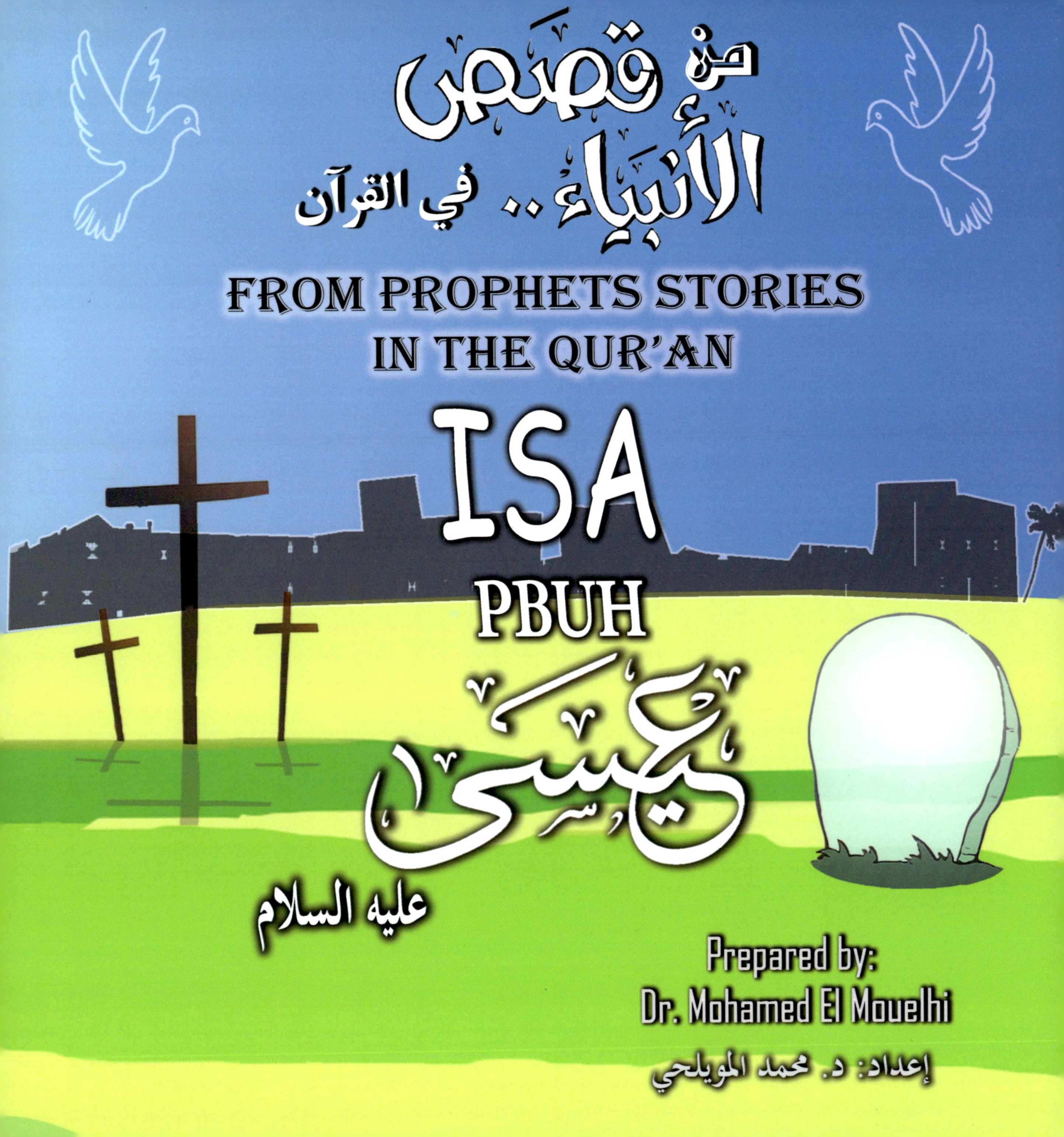

من قصص الأنبياء .. في القرآن

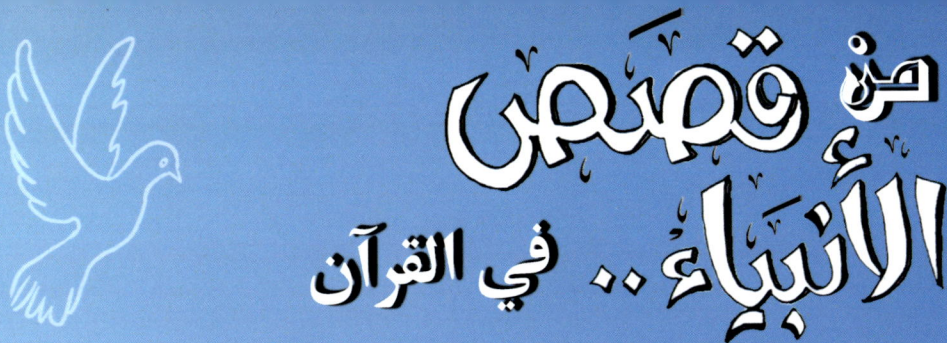

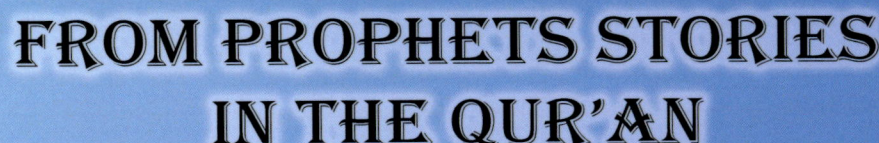

FROM PROPHETS STORIES IN THE QUR'AN

ISA PBUH

عيسى عليه السلام

Prepared by:
Dr. Mohamed El Mouelhi

إعداد: د. محمد المويلحي